You Are an Amazing Girl

A COLLECTION OF STORIES LIVED BY A LITTLE GIRL TO TEACH YOU TO BE BRAVE AND ALWAYS BELIEVE IN YOURSELF.

A MOTIVATIONAL BOOK ABOUT COURAGE, INNER STRENGTH, AND FRIENDSHIP.

JULIA LEE WILSON

A Gift for You!!!

Scan the qr-code

NOW and find out how what it's all about!

SUMMARY

Introduction

Hi, I'm Julia: I'm 11 years old and in sixth grade.

I live in a suburban town with my parents, my sister, and our little dog.

My favorite hobbies are dancing (I dance with my BFF Clare) and music (I play the violin at school).

I like to take long walks in the mountains with my family because I always meet new people that way.

When I was younger, I always felt shy and insecure, but now I am a sunny little girl and very persistent: I do everything to get what I want!

Sometimes my parents like this behavior, especially when I study for good grades at school.

Other times, for example, when I want to organize a small party or a sleepover with my friends at our house, I nag my mum and dad until they give me permission!

I love spending time with my friends, but like you, I don't get along with all the boys and girls in my class. Sometimes I fight with them, but we always make up in the end.

In this book, I will tell you about some adventures I have had that have helped me a lot to overcome my fears and uncertainties.

I would like to make you realize how important it is not to underestimate yourself, to believe in yourself, and to try to bond and socialize with peers.

I hope you will enjoy it and that we can also become BFFs (Best Friend Forever).

Hi,
Julia.

A Special Birthday

Finally! After a year, it was time to think about birthdays again!

This year Serena wanted to organize her birthday outdoors, in the city park, where all the guests would have plenty of games, a basketball court, and a football pitch.

Serena thought this was an excellent idea. In April, after a long winter, who would want to lock themselves in a small room to celebrate a friend's birthday?!

And so she began to organize her tenth birthday in every detail.

The theme of the party was: flowers! So Serena asked her sister to help her make necklaces out of colorful crepe paper flowers. Even the invitations were flower-shaped, with the names of invited friends written on them. She commissioned her mother to buy chips, biscuits, and soft drinks to be eaten under the pavilion.

The day of the party had arrived, and Serena was delighted to see that many of her friends had accepted the invitation: they would have a great time!

She had prepared games, which she thought were very addictive: a game of 'girls against boys' football and a quiz with many questions. She couldn't wait to start.

While waiting for all the guests to arrive, the girls and boys scattered around the park, gathering in small groups. Serena noticed this but thought: "Until all my friends have arrived, I can let them play, then I will call them to start the games I have organized!"

After about half an hour, everyone arrived. Still, she could no longer get her friends and girlfriends together because they were having so much fun playing around the park: little boys were playing five-a-side football, little girls were swinging on swings, and other little girls were doing cartwheels on the basketball court.

No one seemed to care about Serena, and she felt sadder and sadder, almost angry.

Her mother, seeing her saddened, asked her why and she replied: 'No one plays with me, I want all my friends to come here, I am not having fun alone...'.
So Mummy told her to run off and play with the other girls right away and that she could play your games on another occasion, perhaps

during the winter, and added: 'You chose to have your birthday party in the park, so enjoy all this beautiful open space! Go play with your friends".

A little hesitant, he decided to follow his mother's advice. She went to play with the girls in the swing, then decided to shoot some hoops with the boys and began having a lot of fun, completely forgetting about the football game and the quiz.

A piece of music, almost deafening, drew her and the other girls under the pavilion.

All of Serena's friends gathered around her for the souvenir photo.

Mum had prepared a beautiful floral cake ... in keeping with the party theme!

It was a 3-tier meringue cake decorated with colorful sugar flowers and a big white chocolate heart.

Every time Serena looks at that photo, jealously preserved on her bedside table, she thinks back to that beautiful day and wonders: "If I had forced my friends to play the games I had organized, would they have had as much fun?"

Probably not. A party in the park, free to run all over the place, is the best way to have fun after a long week at school!!!

Space intentionally left blank to prevent the
colors running through the text.

Clare's New Passion

Clare and Anna were inseparable friends. They had known each other since kindergarten.

Anna invited Clare to her dance recital: the theatre, the costumes, the music...everything was beautiful, and Clare thought: 'I would like to learn to dance like Anna'. But her friend had already been dancing for four years and trained in the gym three times a week.

So Clare asked her mum to sign her up to dance with Anna. Mum explained that if she signed up, she would have to attend the class every week, even when she didn't feel like it or when her friends went to the park to play and eat ice cream.

Clare began to think about it. Would she enjoy dancing so much that she would give up going to the park with her friends? Anna told her that she sometimes struggled to get out of bed in the morning because of severe pain in her feet and legs. On the other hand, Clare used the children's scooter to move from room to room: would she have endured all those pains?

Yes.

She likes dancing so much. She thought she could put up with it all as long as she could practice and dance with her best friend.

So, the following week her mother enrolled her in the dance studio.

At the end of class, Mum asked if she was happy with the lesson. "Yes, mum, I loved it. I want to come back next week!".

The other girls greeted her with big smiles. They showed her where the changing room was and accompanied her to the gymnasium: how big it was!

The other girls greeted her with big smiles. They showed her where the changing room was and accompanied her to the gymnasium: how big it was!

The teachers started with the warm-up. The girls had to do some stretching and then splits and cartwheels. It didn't seem real to Clare!

She worked hard because she wanted to reach

Anna's level, or at least not make a wrong impression.

As happy the afternoon before ... As sore the following day, Clare woke up all sore but remembered what her friend Anna had told her: 'If your legs hurt in the morning, do some stretching, and the pain will go away'.

So Clare sat down on the carpet in the nursery to stretch her legs.

Mum entered the room and was happy to see that, instead of complaining of pain, Clare was stretching her muscles, as her friend had advised.

In the following months, she intensified her training, going to the gym three times a week, like the best students. Anna was happy that Clare had chosen the same sport as her: they were best friends.

And Clare no longer thought about afternoons in the park, sometimes really boring, but occupied all her free time training for the end-of-year recital.

This time she would also participate. She would not be among the spectators but would take the stage with Anna and the other dancers.

The performance was beautiful, and Clare's parents were very proud of their little girl.

She had learned to sacrifice her free time and playtime for training. And all this training paid off. In just one year, Clare was now the little but great dancer she had always wanted to be.

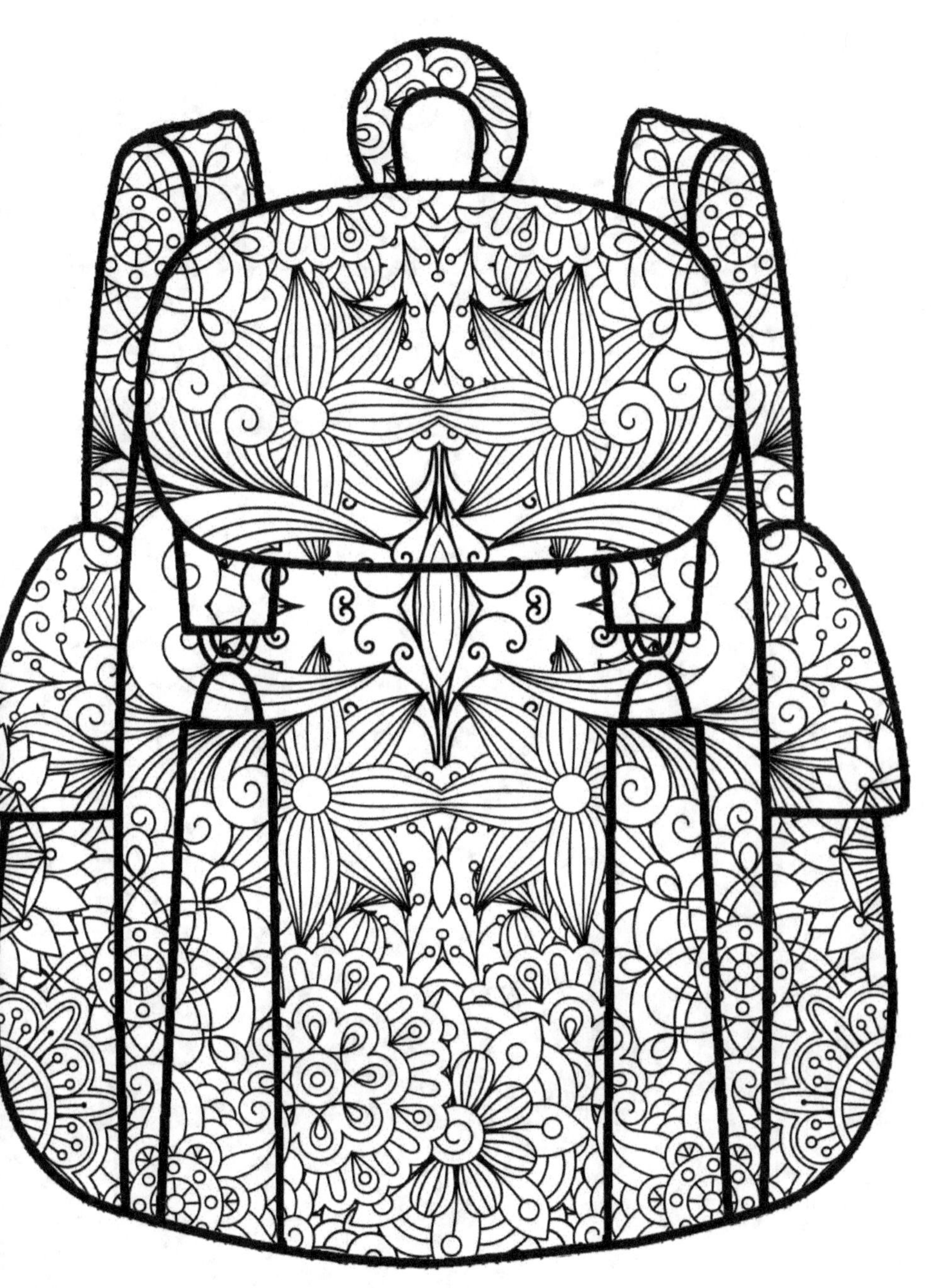

Space intentionally left blank to prevent the colors running through the text.

The Mountain Hike

After three months of continuous school work, the summer holiday was finally announced.

My parents planned a holiday to Africa, but I insisted we take a mountain hike in the Alps.

"Don't worry," I told my family. "We are going to have so much fun."

"We better do, Bianca," said my four years old sister, Mary.

We bought every survival kit we needed, then jumped into the SUV and started the journey.

After several hours we saw the beautiful sight of the Alps Mountain.

"Wow..." the whole family said admiringly.

We went to our hotel and refreshed ourselves. After a nice bath and warm food, we kitted up and started the hike with some other tourists.

The landscape was so enchanting and breathtaking that everyone would frequently pause, taking silent pictures with their minds and cameras before moving on.

After an hour, we all stopped on a flat rock to rest and have a snack. I noticed another girl

from the tour wearing a pink dress.

Her hair was blond: she was beautiful. She seemed to be my age, so I fancied I could be friends with her.

I went to meet her. "Hello, my name is Bianca," I said politely, "what's yours?"

She sized me up with her eyes and didn't reply. Instead, she put on her AirPods and engaged her mobile phone.

I returned to my family, feeling embarrassed and hurt.

"What's wrong?" Mum asked, apparently noticing a change in my mood.

"Nothing," I said.

"Are you sure?"

"Yes, Mum."

She passed me a bar of chocolate, and I chewed it halfheartedly. I felt like a fool; in my mind, I screamed: why on earth did I do that?

After a brief rest, we continued the hike. I wasn't happy anymore, and the mountain view seemed to have lost its charm.

Every time I looked back and sighted the blonde girl, I felt a surge of stupidity and anger.

Suddenly, I felt a hand on my shoulder.

"Hey," Dad said. "I saw what happened back there, don't let it affect your esteem, sweetie. Everyone can't be nice, you know. If it were so, then the world would have been better than this."

"Thanks, Dad." I felt a whole lot better.

Not long after that, dark clouds moved across the sky, and the bright day became dull.

"Looks like another rain is about to begin," the tour guide announced. "Let's start heading back to the hotel now. Tomorrow, we shall continue".

We started returning, and Dad carried Mary on his shoulder while she whined about her sore feet.

Suddenly the rain started, and the ground became treacherously slippery.

"Everyone, stick together," the tour guide said, "and let's move as fast as we can."

I looked ahead and noticed the blonde-haired girl was a little bit away from everyone else. She was getting too close to the side of the ravine.

She was still engaging her mobile phone, even though we were on the move and in the rain.

With her ears plugged like that, I wasn't sure she knew the gravity of our situation.

Without thinking, I started moving toward her.

I wanted to tell her she was getting too close to the fall, but before I could do that, a brilliant flash of lightning struck.

The blonde girl panicked and stumbled; before she knew it, she was falling. I reached out a hand and grabbed her.

The whole crowd gasped, but I was able to pull her upright.

"Are you all right," I asked.

"Yes," she said in shock. "Thank you." She looked down the drop. "But my phone's gone."

"Sorry about that," I said.

"It's fine. Thank you so much."

I looked back and saw everyone applauding me; I blushed as my Dad gave me a little wink.

We changed our wet clothes and drank hot coffee when we reached the hotel.

Mum and Dad were still showing me praises when I heard a knock on the door. I went to get it, and it was the blonde

girl.

"Hi there," she said. "Can I see you? Just for a minute, please."

"Sure."

I told my family I would be back soon, and I followed her.

"I want to apologize for earlier," she said. "I shouldn't have...behaved the way I did."

"It's okay," I said.

"My name is Isabella," she continued awkwardly, "Thank you again for what you did. I am hoping we can be friends?"

"Why not? My name is Bianca, and I'll love to be your friend."

That was the beginning of our friendship.

Even though we live far apart, we still write to each other almost every day to tell each other how the day went!

Space intentionally left blank to prevent the colors running through the text.

How difficult it is to study ...

A week full of classroom tests: who will make it...

Monday maths, Wednesday English, Thursday Italian and Friday...the horrible geography!!!

Anne was very worried because she had not gotten a good grade on the geography test the year before.

"But what is the point of memorizing all the names of the mountains? And those strange cities?" wondered Anne.

She read and read but could not get them into her head.

Mum explained to Anne that as a child, she hated subjects like maths and geometry. She liked reading and writing, but she would never have been a maths teacher!

When she grew up, however, she realized that learning to solve maths problems would allow her to develop her mind and train it to solve other issues, such as programming the air conditioner at home or managing the car's computer.

She explained to Anne that studying was not just memorizing mounds, dates, and various formulas.

"Especially in the first years of school, it is right to study all subjects, from maths to history, from Italian to English, to learn many things, and also to understand what you like," her mother told Anne.

So Anne began to study all subjects, especially those she was less good at, first and foremost geography!

For several days he repeated all the names of the Italian mountains, lakes and rivers. She wrote them down in a little notebook and read them every day before bed.

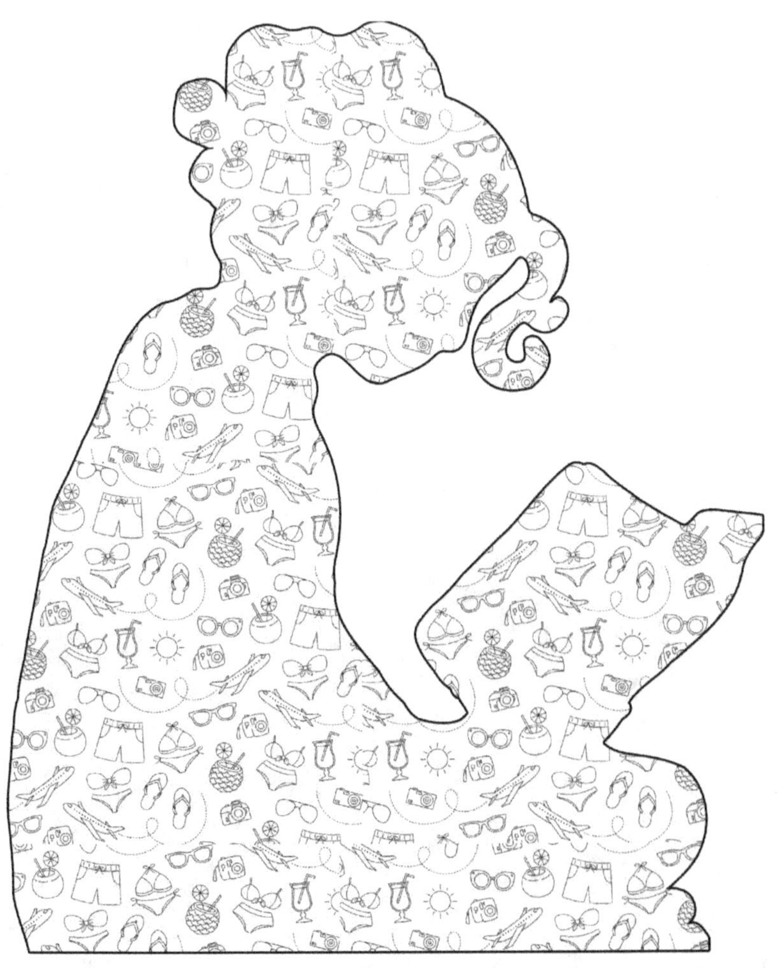

She had seen this method from her older sister.

Anne was very nervous on the test day: would it go well, or would she forget everything, as always?

Yes, it would have been fine!

When the teacher handed over the sheet with the questions, Anne sighed heavily and thought: 'I can do it. I can do it".

She read the questions one by one, imagining the answers in her little head: this time, the test did not seem so complicated!

He began to answer the questions calmly, without panicking. Some she did not know, but she was happy to be able to give so many answers.

The teacher passed by the desks and approached Anne. She asked why she was so smiling; she was constantly agitated during tests. Anne replied that she had prepared well for that class test and that geography no longer frightened her.

After a few days, the teacher handed in the tests: Anne's grade was good this time. She was happy with that grade and couldn't wait to go home and tell her mother about it.

Mum told her that she was very proud of her. Anne had learned that all subjects are essential and must be followed well, even if they are not liked.

She had realized that if you do not study hard, you cannot expect to get good grades. Her new method had led to that goal that seemed unattainable to her.

From that day, Bianca studied more willingly and with ease. The school was even becoming enjoyable and on test days, she enjoyed testing her preparation!!!

Unites we stand, Divided we fall

Once upon a time, many girls and boys studied in a school. It was a well-renowned school, and its reputation was relatively high.

The children were 9 years of age, sharp-minded, and obedient to the teacher, but at times some boys got very stubborn.

The school was big and had many gardens, beautiful trees, and plants with flowers blooming. All the classmates used to roam around these gardens in their free time.

They had fun; they played games such as badminton, volleyball, the high jump, and much more.

However, among these young students were two boys who used to quarrel with others despite their teachers guiding them about friendship.

They never listened.

Those boys were Guenevre and Sarah. Most of the time, the other good students got irritated and distracted and complained about their annoying behavior to the school principal.

One fine day, the teacher announced in the class that a sports competition would be held next week and wanted students to participate actively in all the games.

The teacher explained: "There will be multiple indoor and outdoor athletics games, and you all have to play in teams in a group of sporting events that involves competitive running, jumping, throwing, and walking".

Rania said excitedly, "Wow! That's awesome. I am so excited; I am such a great athlete. I also won last time".

Rania was a lovely child who listened to and respected others. She believed in playing together.

Unfortunately, she was always the target of Guenevre and Sarah.

"You won by cheating; now it's my turn to get the reward" shouted Sarah.

Guenevre laughed and replied: "The tables will rotate towards me this time".

"You always annoy me while playing games", complained Rania to Guenevre and Sarah.

The two mischievous girls replied: "You never give us a chance for our trial, so we annoy you."

The teacher yelled at that moment: "Say sorry, both of you, to Rania, or else we won't play any games in the future, and we won't come into these gardens either".

The teacher tried her best to unite these girls with others, but she failed to bond them, and they always fought badly.

She discussed these naughty students with other faculty as well.

All of them decided to call for a parent-teacher meeting as it's their parent's responsibility to guide their children.

When the parents were called, they also showed concern for the teachers. They were not in their control too.

The teacher also felt sad for the parents and promised she'd train them.

Rania decided to teach them a lesson to forget their differences and come in unity.

The next day, the teacher said, "Let's play an indoor game. We aren't going to gardens today."

The students agreed. Rania intelligently gave an indoor game idea to the teacher.

"Rania has a great idea to share with us; let's hear her out"

She provided her classmates with a bundle of 10 sticks and asked them to break each stick into pieces.

The children broke them very quickly in minutes and then quarreled among themselves again.

"The game isn't over yet, dear students," said the teacher.

"I will be providing you all with the bundle of sticks again, but this time you are not breaking them individually. Instead, break them all together as a bundle, perhaps you all can do," said Rania.

Guenevre said: "It's impossible, how are we supposed to do it"?

"It's hurting my palms. Sorry, I can't play this game", cried Sarah.

The students told the teacher of their failure to break the bundle of sticks despite trying many times.

All of them tried to break the bundle with plenty of force, but the bundle of sticks was tough to break. They were unable to do it at any cost.

The sticks were made of wood, which started hurting the hands of students, and therefore, they all quit the game.

The teacher said, "What does this tell us, Rania? Share it with everyone"

Rania stood up and said, "Breaking every single stick individually was easy for us, but breaking them in a bundle, we could not do.

By staying united, nobody can harm us. If we continue to quarrel, then anyone can quickly defeat us.

Remember, the enemies want to see us weak and drift, so if we part ways by arguing with each other every time, anybody can take this advantage and try their best to annihilate us.

However, seeing us in union and the majority will shake the enemy's confidence, and they will be terrified enough to make any misuse of us".

"Perfectly yes, that's right, Rania," said her teacher proudly.

"Oh, I see that was why you always ask us to bond and make friendships", exclaimed Saim.

Anna pledged: "I want to apologize to my classmates, especially Rania and Sarah. Let's be friends, and we won't be apart anymore."

All the children agreed happily and profoundly.

The teacher added, "I ask that you stay united." Then, the students understood there's power in unity and promised their mentor they would all stay together.

Everyone applauded Rania for her fantastic idea to bring everyone together.

The game taught them a very fruitful and thoughtful lesson; ultimately, the objective was identified clearly.

From this day, in all future events, the students played all the games together, didn't bother others, obeyed the teacher's commands, and became excellent students.

The teacher gave gifts to her entire class, which cheered and uplifted their confidence.

Their parents were very grateful to the teacher.

MORAL:
United we stand, divided we fall.

Like in this story, when the boys fought with each other or annoyed Rania, whether in their games or their studies because of competition, they failed most of the time and ended up only making arguments.

Healthy competition is good but hurting someone physically or their sentiments is inappropriate. We will be more successful if we all stay united and act as a team in doing tasks.

Rania's indoor game idea made children understand that the power of bundles is incomparable to be broken collectively rather than the separate sticks.

So it's better to act like a team rather than degrading and letting others down.

You are an Amazing Girl

Elsa wishes to be a bit taller and skinny and that she has blue eyes. Elsa says while looking in the mirror.

At the same time, her mother tells her that they are getting late for the party and that she should be quick.

"Coming, mom, give me just 5 minutes", she replies.

She quickly sets everything and rushes towards the gate where her sister and parents are waiting for her. Her mother and brother were disappointed by her look.

Her mother tells her that she would've worn the black dress, while her sister tells her that she looks even smaller in her shoes.

She looks at herself and feels terrible.

"Should I go and change?" She asks them.

"No need to change; you look perfect," her father says. "But Mary and mom didn't like it, Dad?" she says.

He looks at both of them and tells her that she shouldn't listen to them; she is perfect in her beautiful way, and they are getting late.

They all should go and sit in the car.

Everybody listens to him and sits in the car. They were going to the engagement ceremony of their dad's friend's son.

They reach there in an hour. They all welcome them warmly.

"Where's Emily? Can I meet her?" Elsa asks. "Yes, dear, she is in the make-up room. She was waiting for you.

Go and meet her," the bride's mother says.

Elsa moved towards the garden and was looking for the make-up room.

"What are you looking for, pretty lady?", she hears a voice.

She turns back. "Are you talking to me?", she asks shockingly.

"I don't see another lady here. Of course, I am talking to you", he says.

"Oh, it's Elsa. I am Emily's Friend. Where is the make-up room?", she asks.

"Hey, Elsa, it's Harry. Do you always look this pretty? Or's it the white color that makes you look this good? Let me take you to the make-up room",
he says.

"Pretty and I? You're good at lying, man. Yes, take me there", she replies.

They kept on talking on their way. They saw an injured cat.

So, Elsa rushed to her and held her in her arms.

She tore a piece of her scarf and covered that cat's paw.

She made sure the cat was doing okay; she left the cat on the ground, and the cat started walking a bit normally now.

Harry was looking at all this.

He was shocked that Elsa tore her clothes for the cat's sake, and she still thinks she is not beautiful.

He tells her natural beauty lies in caring for people and having a good heart.

Elsa still doesn't listen to him and tells him that we all know nobody cares how caring or loving you all are.

She says everybody craves the prettiest face, a perfect body, and flawless skin.

Harry is very disappointed by her perspective and tells her that she is surrounded by very pessimistic people who are all going nowhere in life.

Elsa doesn't get him and asks if he prefers a pretty face or a pretty heart. Harry gets a bit angry and tells her when we will be looking for faces.

People would like our outer beauty for some years. And like everything else, it would fade one day.

But a beautiful heart would remain forever.

The person who would choose her for her looks would be bored of you some days, but the one who would fall for her heart would always make her feel special.

He tells her that she shouldn't get fooled and that she is a beautiful human.

And it took him hardly five minutes to see her beautiful heart. It makes Elsa teary.

"I needed this harry. Thank you so much", she says.

"No thank you speech, Emily is waiting for you. Let's go", he laughs.

She clears her eyes, smiles back, and they both move towards the make-up room.

Space intentionally left blank to prevent the colors running through the text.

Julia's Journey

BRRRRRING, BRRRRRRING.... Julia's alarm is ringing.

It's six in the morning. Julia wakes up every morning at six, even on weekends and holidays.

She always wants to practice before school.

She is an award-winning violinist, and she's only in grade 8.

Julia is determined to be the best, and she is. She dedicates every morning to practice because she was taught if you want to get better, you must be better.

Julia started playing the violin when she was just 5 years old and hasn't been able to put it down since.

Each day she gets better and better. She never skips a practice.

Julia goes to Pinewood Secondary school.

Her favorite subject is music. She's also a member of the elite jazz and classical bands.

Julia's two best friends, Maggie and Drew, are her biggest supporters. They don't have a musical bone in their bodies and think Julia is a superstar.

"Hey Julia, how was your weekend?" Maggie asks as Julia arrives at school.

"It was fun. I spent most of it..." before Julia could finish her sentence, she heard Drew and Maggie shout, "Practising?"

"You know me well," Julia said.

It was no secret Julia put her violin practice above everything else. It has and will always be her top priority.

She was called to the principal's office on Thursday.

Julia was worried. "What did I do wrong?", She asks the teacher who is accompanying her out of the classroom.

Julia opens the principal's office door and is delighted to see balloons and a bouquet. There are also his parents. She is perplexed.

"What is all this?" Julia asks.

The principal explains Julia has been selected to join Providence School of the Arts.

It was a much bigger school, focused solely on music and drama.

It had been a dream of Julia's to attend but was

one she never thought would become a reality.

She should be happy, but she was a little scared. This school was two towns away.

There were many more students and a lot who were good at music.

Julia wondered if she would still be the best violinist.

To make matters even scarier for Julia, she started the next day.

BRRRRRRRRRING BRRRRRRING... Julia's alarm startles her awake.

This morning she woke up at 5:30 to get an extra half hour of practice before heading to her new school.

Julia was worried, stressed and scared. She couldn't focus.

She needed to take two buses to get to Providence.

When she arrived, Julia couldn't believe how big it was.

Her fear of not being good enough and not being the best tripled.

Inside she found out there were 15 violinists. At her old school, she was the only violinist.

She rushed home that night and practiced for three more hours.

She even skipped dinner.

Julia was exhausted, but she couldn't stand that she wasn't the best anymore.

She spent the next two weeks waking up extra early, going to school, and then heading home to practice even more.

Still, she didn't feel like she was better than the other top violinists at Providence.

She wasn't happy. She was frustrated and putting herself down.

And worst of all, she was starting to dislike the violin. She had loved this instrument since she was a kid. It brought her joy and pride and sometimes even helped her feel courageous.

Julia had always had a violin in her hand, and now she was putting it away.

"I'm done!" Julia told her parents, "I'm not even good anyway."

Julia's parents were shocked. They couldn't believe their little girl, who had always loved playing, didn't want to do it anymore.

"If I can't be the best, there is no point in me playing at all", Julia said as she closed the violin case and shoved it under her bed.

Four weeks passed, and Julia only played the violin when she had to in school.

Jillian was one of Providence's top players and started noticing how unhappy Julia looked when she played in class.

"Hey!" Jillian called out to Julia after school, "are you okay? I've noticed you don't seem very happy while playing anymore."

"Well, it's probably because I'm not good at it anymore," Julia said disappointedly.

"Julia, you're one of the best violinists I've heard at this school!" Jillian admitted. She was stunned to think Julia didn't know the same.

Hearing those words made Julia feel even sadder. It was a shocking reminder of the years of hard work she has put into her craft.

"You think I'm good?" Julia asked.

"Yes, when you first started here, we were shocked at how good you were.

We were so happy to have you join us."

That also confused Julia, "Wait! You were happy I was good?"

"Of course," Jillian said, "we love having the best talent here."

That's when Julia realized she had been looking at all this wrong.

She realized she didn't have to be the best. It should have been enough to be around the best.

Getting invited to Providence should have been proof enough that she was the best.

"You're right! Wow, I should have been proud. I am excellent."

Julia gave Jillian the tightest hug.

Julia was excited to get home and play for the first time in a long time.

She was amazing and now she was able to see it that way.

Julia's journey may not have been perfect, but she ended up in the right place.

MORAL

Julia learned being perfect isn't what's important. She learned to believe in herself and never give up.

She learned you can't always be the best, but you can be inspired by others to do better.

The Best Gift!

Soon it will be Christmas: pandoro, holidays, snow and ... presents!

This year the teacher had a great idea: each pupil would bring a gift, and then the teacher would distribute one of these gifts to each child.

The only rule: the gift had to be created with one's own hands and not bought.
Sylvia was overjoyed. She had the chance to create the handicraft with her hands and give it to a friend. In return, she would receive a gift prepared by another child.

Sylvia had no doubts: she would create a beautiful gnome out of wool and cardboard to attach to the Christmas tree. She had seen some examples on the Internet and wanted to make one.

So she procured all the materials:
- a ball of white wool
- a piece of red cardboard;
- some glue;
- a pair of scissors.

She asked her mother if she could help her.

"Sure, Sylvia, explain what we have to do", Mummy told her, smiling.

"First, you have to form a pompom with the

wool", Sylvia explained.

Then Sylvia rolled the wool between her fingers, tied it in the center, and cut the edges.

"Then, mum, we have to draw a triangle in the red cardboard and close it with glue", said Sylvia.

We've done it!

"Finally, we must glue the hat on top of the pom pom and attach a green ribbon."

We've done it!

Sylvia was very proud of her gnome: it had come out well!

On the day of the gift exchange, she brought her gnome to school and placed it on the teacher's desk.

There were lots of beautiful crafts: paper trains,

woolen sheep, cardboard handbags!!!

Sylvia's best friend, Claudia, had created a stocking for the Befana's sweets by sewing an old sock.

She was very proud of her handiwork because she had made it herself.

Claudia lived in a low-income family with her 3 little brothers, mum, and dad.

The teacher arranged the crafts next to each other and, calling the pupils in alphabetical order, distributed all the crafts, one to each pupil.

Lara, a bit bossy and obnoxious, protested because she said she had received the ugliest present.

"I'll throw it away, teacher...I don't like this handiwork," she said.
It was Claudia's stocking.

Poor Claudia began to cry. She was sorry that her classmate did not like her handiwork.

Then Sylvia, who had received a beautiful white woolen sheep instead, asked the teacher if she could exchange it for Claudia's stocking

"I like that very much. I know it was made with love", said Sylvia, "and when I look at it hanging on the tree, I will never forget my friend Claudia".

And so, Sylvia exchanged the sheep for the Claudia's stocking.

Claudia immediately ran to hug Sylvia and told her: "You will be my BFF, and you will always be my BFF!".

Then the teacher asked the meaning of that

word, and Sylvia, looking at Claudia, said: "BFF means we will be Best Friends Forever!"

PS: if you also want to create a cute gnome, follow Sylvia's instructions!

You can change the color of the carded wool and thus obtain  different gnomes. Use the classic colors: whit